Copyright © 2025 Jennifer Jones
All copyright laws and rights reserved.
Published in the U.S.A.
For more information, email info@ninjalifehacks.tv
Paperback ISBN: 978-1-63731-975-8
Hardcover ISBN: 978-1-63731-977-2
eBook ISBN: 978-1-63731-976-5

Find the Easter Bunny on Strike lesson plans at ninjalifehacks.tv

The next day in their classroom,
a letter came in pink.
It smelled like grass and jellybeans
and made the teacher blink.

I hide your eggs in trees and shrubs, in spots not meant for me. I'm climbing walls and slipping slides, and landing clumsily!

You hand me maps and hush your voice,
"You must be sly tonight!"
But I'm just a bunny with fluffy feet,
I trip more than I fight!

Miss Daisy said, "Let's make it right and help the Easter Bunny too. We'll fix the hunt with simple rules and make space for a bunny crew!"

They marked soft grass with signs and flags
and made each egg hunt clear.
They built a lounge with carrot juice
and bunny treats each year.

Design Your Bunny-Friendly Egg Hunt!

Help keep the bunnies safe and happy.

Favorite hiding spot: _____

Bunny break snack: _____
_____

Easy rule for your hunt: _____
_____
_____

Draw something from your Bunny-Friendly Egg Hunt here!